Baltimore

MARYLAND

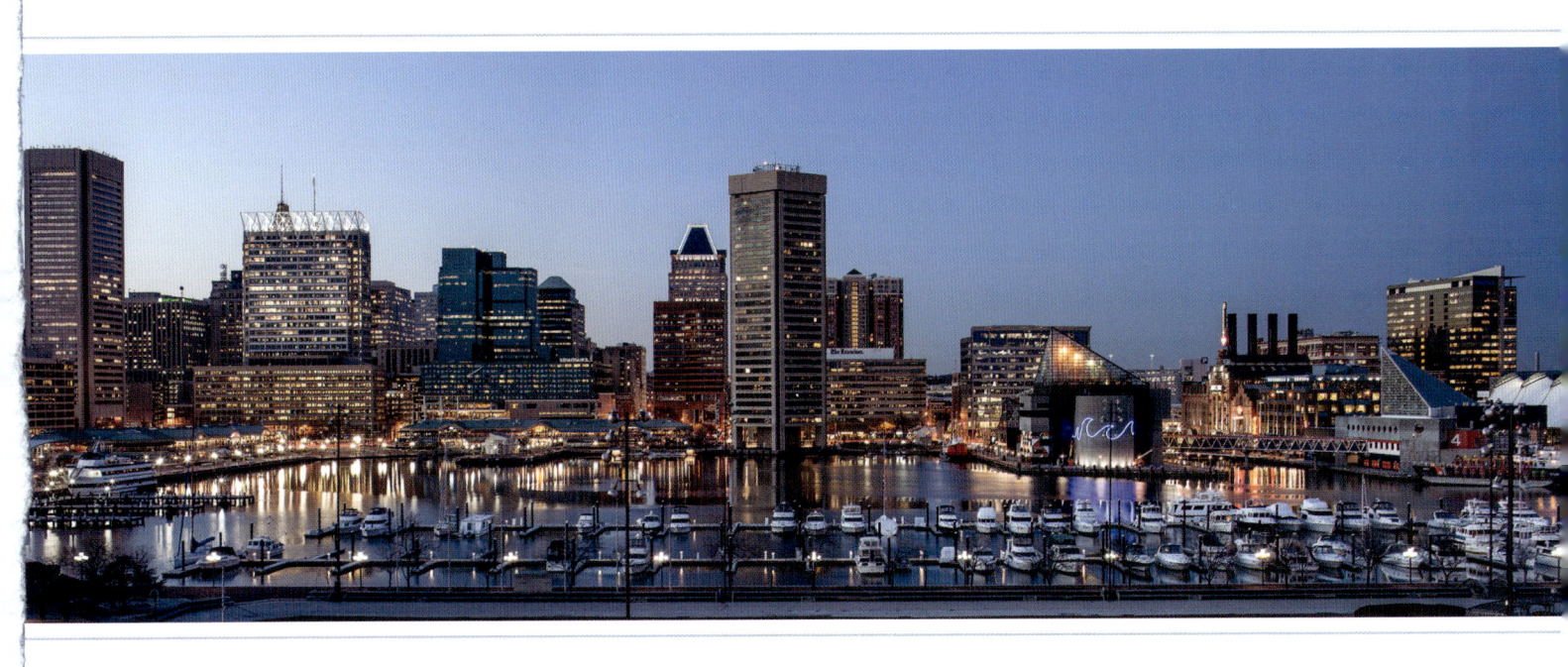

A PHOTOGRAPHIC PORTRAIT

PHOTOGRAPHY BY

Alan Gilbert

NARRATIVE BY

Brooke McDonald

TWIN LIGHTS PUBLISHERS | ROCKPORT, MASSACHUSETTS

Copyright © 2016 by
Twin Lights Publishers, Inc.

All rights reserved. No part of this book may be reproduced in any form without written permission of the copyright owners. All images in this book have been reproduced with the knowledge and prior consent of the artists concerned and no responsibility is accepted by producer, publisher, or printer for any infringement of copyright or otherwise, arising from the contents of this publication. Every effort has been made to ensure that credits accurately comply with information supplied.

First published in the
United States of America by:

Twin Lights Publishers, Inc.
Rockport, Massachusetts 01966
Telephone: (978) 546-7398
www.twinlightspub.com

ISBN: 978-1-934907-43-6

10 9 8 7 6 5 4 3 2 1

(*opposite*)
Water Taxi

(*frontispiece*)
Skyline

(*jacket front*)
Skyline

(*jacket back*)
Baltimore City Hall and
Bromo-Seltzer Tower

Images on pages 8, 11, 13, 14, and 15 of the Washington Monument are used with the permission of The Mount Vernon Place Conservancy.

Images of the George Peabody Library and Johns Hopkins University are used with permission.

Book design by:
SYP Design & Production, Inc.
www.sypdesign.com

Printed in China

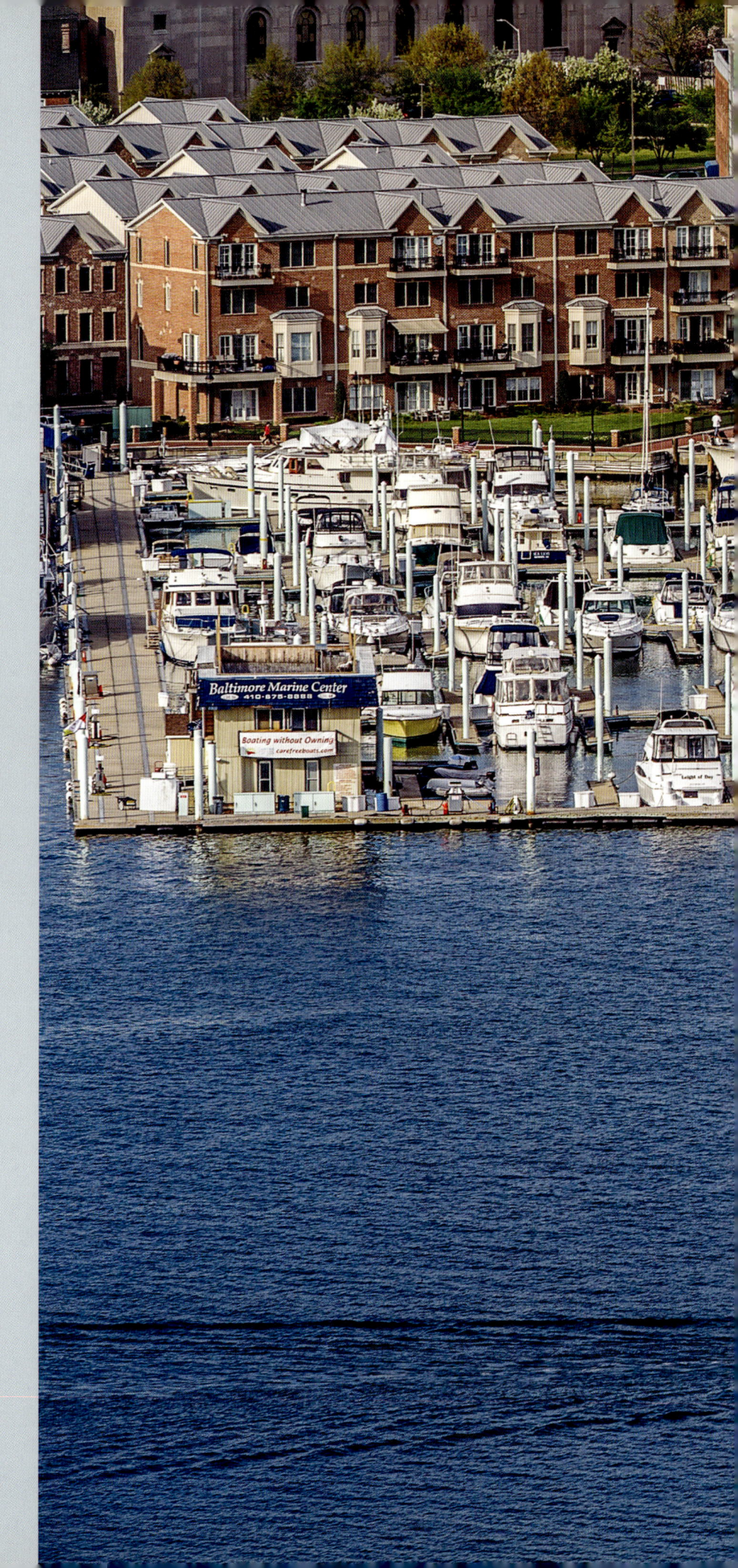

Baltimore is a city that never ceases to surprise—whether you live here your whole life or visit for a day—and it's a strikingly beautiful place from the soaring dome of City Hall to the panoramas of the Inner Harbor at twilight. It's a city full of history and culture, quirky and idiosyncratic with its own one-of-a-kind personality. It's a city of innovation—the birthplace of the national anthem, the railroad, and Babe Ruth—and it celebrates those achievements with monuments and museums that bring the city's story to life.

Baltimore celebrates American independence with the Washington Monument in awe-inspiring Mount Vernon Place, a majestic tribute to the United States' first president which Baltimoreans love to point out was the first in the country. The War of 1812 and the Battle of Baltimore on September 13-14, 1814 were pivotal moments in American history that still loom large in the city's psyche.

At Fort McHenry you can look out to the harbor where British war ships bombed the fort and fought through the night and Francis Scott Key, imprisoned on a Royal Navy ship, watched for "the Star Spangled Banner" at dawn. You can visit the tiny house where Mary Pickersgill stitched that enormous battle flag and imagine the relief of the city as you walk the Belgian block streets of Fells Point.

Other key moments in Baltimore history include the Civil War, the Baltimore Fire of 1904, the Civil Rights Movement, and the unrest of 2015. Take a walk anywhere in the city and learn about all of these and more.

Whatever your passion, there's a museum for you in Baltimore. You'll find arms and armor at the Walters Art Museum, the largest collection of Matisse in the world at the Baltimore Museum of Art, the largest collection of Tiffany glass at Evergreen House. The B&O Railroad Museum has an unparalleled collection of trains displayed in the actual Roundhouse of America's first railroad. There are museums of ships, submarines, streetcars, and firetrucks. Even museums dedicated to comics and lacrosse.

Once the second largest port of entry in the nation, Baltimore is truly a city of immigrants with strong ethnic communities maintaining their traditions today. The Jewish Museum of Maryland invites you to explore historic synagogues and learn about Jewish culture, around the corner from the famous delis on Lombard Street. You are in the home of Irish immigrants who moved here to escape the Great Famine at the Irish Workers Museum. There are golden onion domes of Ukrainian and Polish churches, neighborhoods full of ethnic flair like Little Italy and Greektown, and neighborhoods like Hampden with its very own "Bawlmer" flair.

Baltimore does indeed surprise, as visitors remark who come here knowing only the Orioles, the Ravens, and "The Wire." It's an all-American city, a creative, sometimes crazy place, and a marvelous place to visit or call home.

Baltimore City Hall (*opposite and pages 6–7*)

Baltimore's mayor and City Council have conducted business from this magnificent Baroque Revival building since 1875. Designed by then 22-year-old George A. Frederick, with an iron dome by famed railway-bridge engineer Wendel Bollman, City Hall has seen it all, from peaceful moments to public protests.

Mount Vernon Place *(above)*

The Washington Monument rises behind this beautiful square in Mount Vernon Place, named for George and Martha Washington's home in Virginia. Surrounded by lush trees, water splashes into the pool from Grace Turnbull's Naiad. This 1932 fountain by the Baltimore artist was added in 1962.

Lafayette Monument *(opposite)*

The dashing Marquis de Lafayette sits astride his prancing horse in this bronze by Andrew O'Connor. Installed in front of the Washington Monument in 1924, the statue honors the French hero of the American Revolution for coming to America's aid in 1777 and US support of France in 1917.

Mount Vernon Place

The Stafford Hotel was the height of elegance when it opened in 1894 and you can still see the hotel's name painted on the building, which now houses apartments. F. Scott Fitzgerald, Katharine Hepburn, and Rosa Ponselle were all regular guests of the Stafford Hotel.

Mount Vernon Place

A pink and white palette dominates this square designed by Carrère and Hastings in the 1920s, resplendent with flowering trees and marble balustrades, before the Washington Monument. At center is one of Baltimore's most beloved statues, *Sea Urchin* by Edward Berge, depicting an exuberant nymph atop a sea urchin.

War Memorial

This massive Neo Classical building, flanked by huge, limestone sea horses, was built in the 1920s to commemorate Maryland soldiers who died in World War I. Today, it honors all Marylanders who died in the course of duty in the twentieth century.

Washington Monument

Baltimoreans have always been proud that theirs was the first monument to honor George Washington. Designed by Robert Mills, its cornerstone was laid on July 4, 1815. Mills later designed the US Capitol. The monument is surrounded by glamorous Mount Vernon Place, including the Peabody Institute.

Bust of George Washington *(above)*

This bust of George Washington greets visitors as they enter the base of the Washington Monument to climb up the interior. The monument's board described it as a "Colossal Bust" when they bought it in 1834. Copied after the original by Italian sculptor Giuseppe Ceracchi, the bust weighs 1,000 pounds.

Washington Monument *(opposite)*

Visitors love to climb to the lookout of Washington Monument, which offers panoramic views of the city in all directions. The trip to the top is not for claustrophobics or those who fear heights. It's 227 steps to climb up the cramped spiral staircase, about 145 feet from the ground.

KATYŃ 1940

Bolton Hill *(above and right)*

Bolton Hill is an elegant neighborhood of gracious homes, tree-lined boulevards and parks, featuring historic monuments, including this one of Francis Scott Key, author of "The Star-Spangled Banner," offering his anthem to the brilliant Columbia. The stylish nineteenth-century Beethoven Apartments add contrast to the area's neighborhood's row houses.

National Katyn Memorial *(opposite)*

The gold leaf glows on this sculpture by Andrew Pitynski in the heart of trendy Harbor East. Look closer and you will find figures representing the Polish victims massacred by the Soviets in the Katyn Forest in 1940 and other Polish heroes, a tribute to Baltimore's strong Polish population.

Canton Waterfront

The onion domes of St. Michael the Archangel Ukrainian Catholic Church add an Old World flair to the skyline over Canton. Founder John O'Donnell moved here in 1785 and made his fortune trading with China. Named for its sister port in China, Canton remains a hot spot for boaters.

Belvidere Terrace

Magnificent "Queen Anne" townhouses line both sides of the 1000 block of Calvert Street. Built in the 1880s, the 22 houses here were designed by architects Wyatt & Sperry with an assortment of facades but similar interior layouts. After years as apartments, many are being restored as single-family homes.

Brewers Hill *(top)*

From the 1880s to the 1970s, the National Brewing Co. and Gunther Brewery did, indeed, brew beer in these enormous red-brick breweries on the Hill. Today, they are home to tech firms, shops and apartments, overlooking Canton Waterfront Park and Tindeco Marina.

The Natty Boh Tower *(bottom)*

National Bohemian Beer or "Natty Boh" has been a Baltimore favorite since the National Brewing Co. began making it in 1885 and its mascot "Mr. Boh" is a Baltimore icon. Mr. Boh winks here above Brewers Hill, which has also adopted the National Bohemian slogan "the Land of Pleasant Living."

Bromo-Seltzer Tower *(opposite)*

Head-ache remedy inventor Isaac Emerson was also a master advertiser. In 1911 he built this tower with an enormous Bromo-Seltzer clock face. Styled after the Palazzo Vecchio in Florence, the tower originally featured a 51-foot cobalt blue Bromo-Seltzer bottle. It was Baltimore's tallest building until 1923.

Fort McHenry

This roll-on-roll-off car transport looms large in front of Fort McHenry, much as the British fleet must have looked to the Americans defending Baltimore on September 13, 1814, during the War of 1812. While imprisoned on a British war ship in the harbor, Francis Scott Key composed *The Star-Spangled Banner.*

Fort McHenry

The waters by Fort McHenry are a great place to sail and races like this thrill from spring to fall. Part of the National Park Service today, Fort McHenry has served many roles over its history from Civil War prison for Southern sympathizers to a military hospital in World War I.

Fort Carroll

Robert E. Lee was an engineer in the U.S. Army when he designed Fort Carroll to protect Baltimore in 1847. Fortunately for the city, the fort never saw battle and the Army abandoned it in 1921. Developers have longed to build a casino here but for now birds rule.

Harborplace (top)

Mention Baltimore and most people think of Harborplace, as painted here by local artist Crystal Moll. Opened in 1980 and developed by the Rouse Company, Harborplace was the centerpiece of Mayor William Donald Schaefer's revitalization of Baltimore. Eighteen million visitors came the very first year.

Pierce's Park (left)

Sculptures and native plants beckon you to touch and play and experience all sorts of wonderful art and nature in this compact park on Pier Five. Built in 2012, in memory of businessman Pierce Flanigan III, the park is a favorite Inner Harbor spot for families.

10 Light Street (opposite)

This 34-story art deco skyscraper was the tallest building in Maryland when it was built for the Baltimore Trust Company in 1929. Most recently known as the Bank of America Building, 10 Light Street is now the address for more than 400 modern apartments and an enormous gym.

World Trade Center *(opposite)*

The World Trade Center is the tallest regular pentagonal building in the world, dwarfing surrounding structures and the colorful "Chessie" paddle boats below. Designed by world-renowned architect I.M. Pei, this landmark was completed in 1977. The 27th-floor Observation Level offers spectacular city views.

Christopher Columbus Statue *(above)*

With Italian flags waving, the Italian explorer who "discovered America" gazes east to neighboring Little Italy and beyond. President Ronald Reagan and Mayor William Donald Schaefer dedicated this monument in 1984, a tribute to both Columbus and Baltimore's proud Italian-American community.

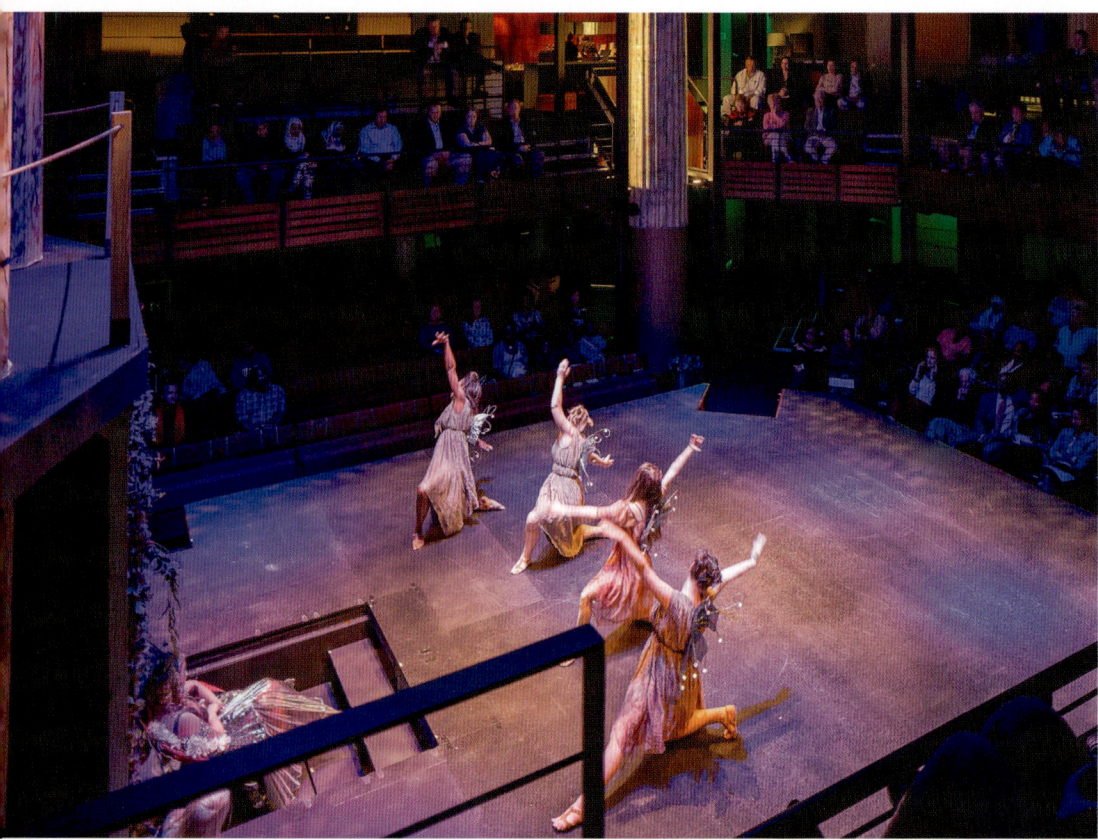

Meyerhoff Symphony Hall *(top)*

Home to the Baltimore Symphony Orchestra since 1982, the Meyerhoff is acclaimed for its stellar acoustics and seats over 2,400. The hall is named for Joseph Meyerhoff, president of the "BSO" from 1965 to 1983 and a driving force in creating this world-class hall for the world-class Baltimore Symphony.

Chesapeake Shakespeare *(bottom)*

A Midsummer's Night Dream is on stage at Chesapeake Shakespeare's own version of the Globe Theater. Founded in 2002, Chesapeake Shakespeare moved to the Mercantile Trust Building in 2014 after it transformed the huge lobby into its authentic Shakespearean theater to stage the playwright's great works.

Maryland Institute College of Art

"MICA" has been educating artists in Baltimore since 1826 and the striking Brown Center, seen here aglow, thrust the institute into the digital age when it opened in 2004. This was the first new addition to the campus in over 100 years, designed by Ziger/Snead and Charles Brickbauer.

Maryland Science Center

Full-size replicas of dinosaur skeletons roam in this massive hall of the Maryland Science Center, delighting aspiring paleontologists and their parents with exhibits that are designed to be touched and experienced. You can dig for fossils and stand in a dinosaur's footprint. The goal is to make science fun.

Maryland Science Center

Prominently situated at the south-west corner of the Inner Harbor, the Maryland Science Center has been inspiring visitors to explore science since 1976. Dinosaurs rule in the wing to the right. There's an IMAX theater and planetarium plus scientific experiments performed on this waterfront plaza.

Walters Art Museum *(top and bottom)*

This "Chamber of Wonders" takes you back in time to the home of a seventeenth-century Dutch collector, with art and artifacts from around the world, displayed from floor to ceiling. The Walters also boasts a remarkable collection of arms and armor from Europe, Turkey, and Japan.

Walters Art Museum *(above and right)*

Henry Walters built this stunning, two-tiered courtyard to display his collection of classical sculptures. In 1909, he opened its doors for the public to enjoy the marvelous works of art he and his father William Walters had collected. Today, the Walters is regarded as one the world's great museums.

Baltimore Museum of Art *(top and bottom)*

Founded in 1914, the Baltimore Museum of Art moved to this magnificent building, adjoining the Johns Hopkins campus, in 1929. Designed by John Russell Pope after a Roman temple, the "BMA" as it's known today, features over 95,000 works of art and the largest collection of Matisse in the world.

Baltimore Museum of Art

This light-filled gallery is a wonderful place to contemplate *The Thinker* by Auguste Rodin. One of only 21 authorized casts of this size and given to the museum in 1930, *The Thinker* originally sat outside the museum's entrance. It was relocated here in 1971.

American Visionary Art Museum

(top and bottom)

This unique museum has been dazzling visitors inside and out since it moved to Key Highway in Federal Hill in 1995. Founded by visionary Rebecca Hoffberger, it celebrates self-taught artists, such as Mr. Imagination's *Throne*, holding court in this imaginative exhibit.

American Visionary Art Museum

At-risk youth created this mosaic of mirrors, pottery, glass, and cobalt-blue bottoms of Noxzema bottles. Parked below is everyone's favorite bus, *Gallery-A-Go-Go* by Nancy Josephson. Vollis Simpson's *Giant Whirligig* spins nearby in all different directions, depending on which way the wind is blowing.

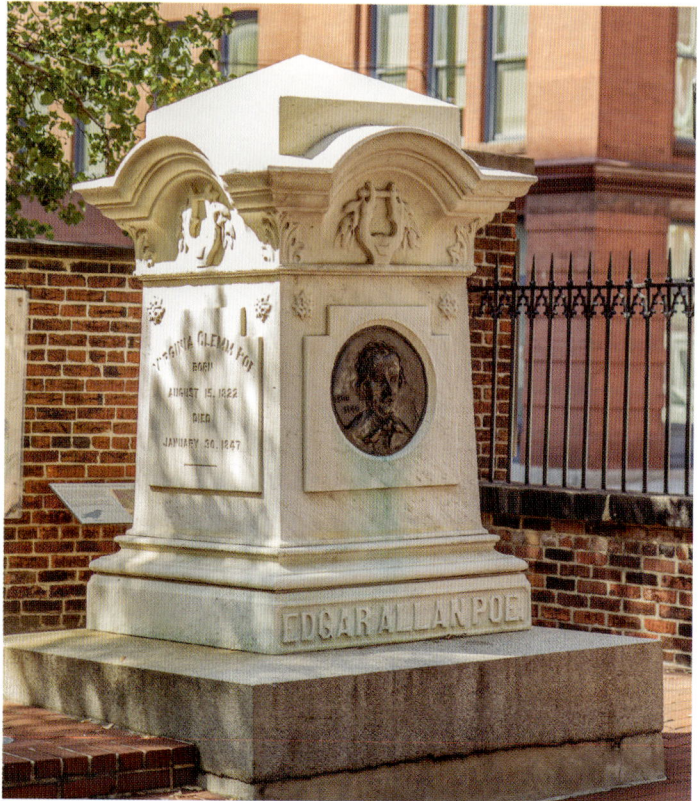

Edgar Allen Poe Statue (above)

This bronze of the great American writer by Sir Moses Ezekiel is a favorite sculpture in the plaza of the University of Baltimore School of Law. Early in his career, Poe lived in Baltimore and his father's family came from here. Baltimoreans have long claimed him for their own.

Edgar Allen Poe Memorial and Gravesite (left)

In 1849, at the age of 40, Edgar Allan Poe died in Baltimore under circumstances that remain a mystery today. His body was moved to a gravesite beside this memorial in 1875, paid for by a fund raised by Poe fans. Internationally, this is one of Baltimore's most well-known sites.

Baltimore Streetcar Museum
(above and right)

You can touch, sit in, and even ride streetcars like these at this gem of a museum. Streetcars ruled in Baltimore from the 1880s to the end of World War II and the fleet here represents many different technologies, including the car that made the very last run in 1963.

B&O Railroad Museum *(above)*

This B&O locomotive is decorated with black bunting, flags, swags, and a portrait of President Abraham Lincoln, replicating the trains that transported Lincoln's body from Washington, D.C. to Springfield, Illinois after his assassination in 1865. The museum's collection includes many trains from the Civil War.

Irish Railroad Workers Museum *(left)*

Irish immigrants lived in these row houses and worked at the B&O Railroad facilities next door. This museum at 918 and 920 Lemmon Street explores their experience in the late 1840s as they fled Ireland's Great Famine. There's a great Irish Heritage Walk in the neighborhood to stroll, as well.

B&O Railroad Museum

This is the actual Roundhouse for the Baltimore & Ohio Railroad where mechanics would work on passenger cars, and the sixty-foot turntable still works today. Baltimore and the B&O take pride in being "the birthplace of American railroading." Today, this is one of the greatest train collections in the world.

Baltimore Museum of Industry
(above and left)

The "BMI" celebrates Baltimore inventions and innovations with exhibits such as this one of Dr. George Bunting's Pharmacy and soda fountain, where Dr. Bunting began selling his revolutionary Noxzema skin cream in 1914. Dr. Bunting's company became cosmetics powerhouse Noxell Corp., now part of Procter & Gamble Co.

Baltimore Museum of Industry
(opposite, top and bottom)

Created from found industrial objects, David Hess's bold sculpture *Working Point*, pays homage to Baltimore's manufacturing heritage, commanding the center of the BMI's brick terrace, overlooking the waterfront just beyond. The museum was originally the site of the old Platt Oyster Cannery.

45

USS Constellation *(above and left)*

Here, on the gun deck of the USS *Constellation*, you can imagine the roar of the cannons and smell of gunpowder, as you touch and feel the guns and ropes of this historic 1854 vessel. The captain and his officers took their meals in this elegant dining room or "mess."

Lady Maryland *(opposite)*

Painted in traditional pink and green, the *Lady Maryland* is hauled on a marine railway at Frederick Douglass-Isaac Meyers Maritime Park. A replica of a Chesapeake Bay "pungy" schooner from the 1800s, she sails as part of the Living Classroom's fleet, the only pungy in the world today.

Pride of Baltimore II *(opposite)*

This replica of a Baltimore clipper serves as an ambassador for Baltimore, Maryland, and the United States as she sails around the world. From the Revolutionary War through the War of 1812, clippers were a favorite of privateers and merchants for their speed and prowess in battle and trade.

USS Constellation *(top)*

A water taxi cuts past the bow of the USS *Constellation* in the heart of the Inner Harbor. The 1854 sloop of war adds historic flair to Harborplace and the waterfront, a majestic reminder of Baltimore's maritime past and a great place to learn about American history and the sea.

Sail Baltimore *(bottom)*

The British Royal Navy's HMS *Argyll* looms over a water taxi as it pulls into Fells Point during the celebration of the two-hundredth anniversary of the War of 1812. Since Operation Sail in 1975, Baltimore has been a regular port of call for tall ships and international navy vessels.

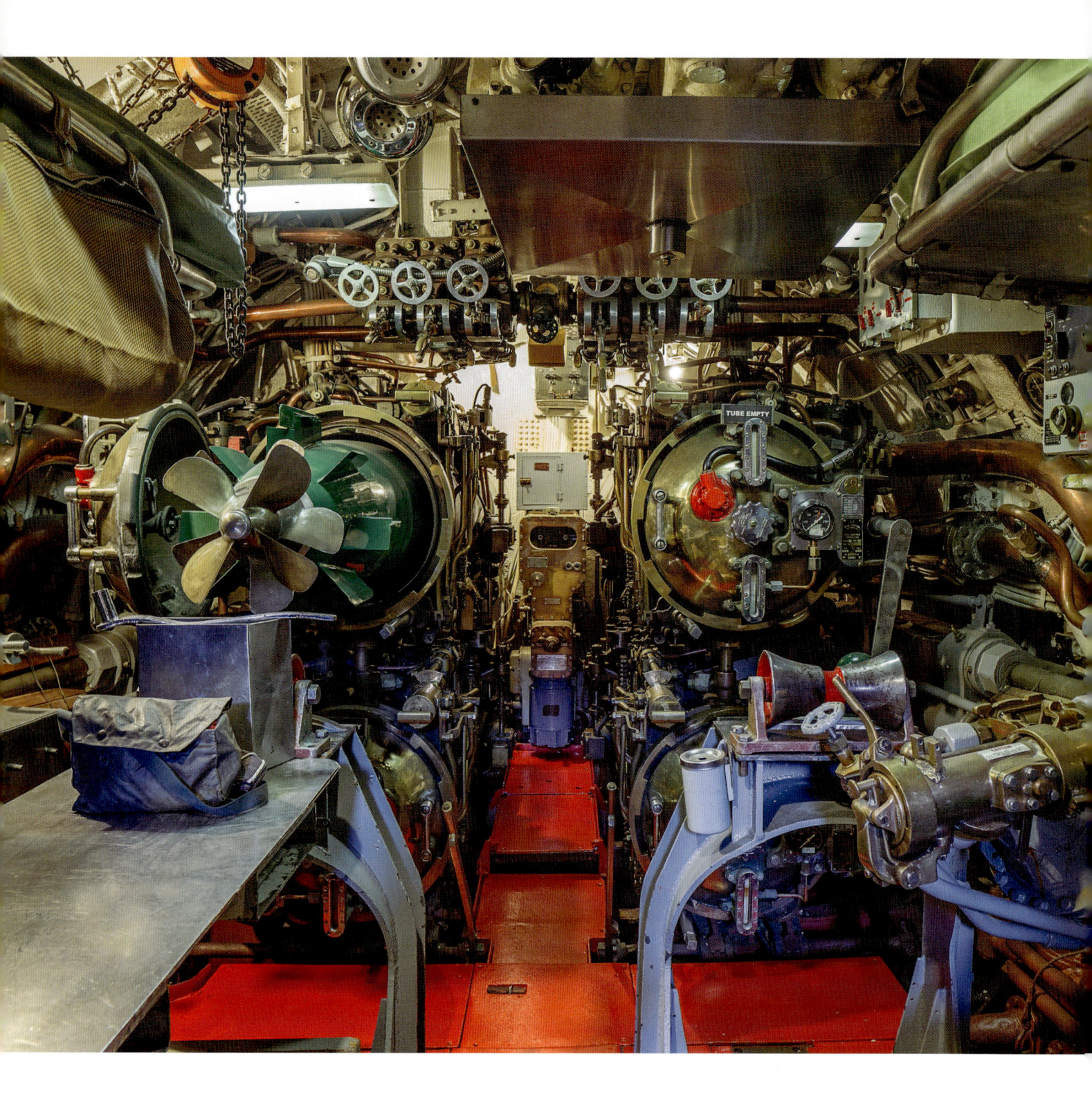

USS Torsk *(above)*

This is the aft torpedo room of the USS *Torsk*, the submarine which sank the very last enemy ship destroyed by the US Navy in World War II. Today, the *Torsk* is open for visitors as part of Historic Ships in Baltimore. You can even spend the night aboard the *Torsk*.

USCGC Taney *(opposite top)*

US Coast Guard Cutter *Taney* is the last ship still afloat to witness the Japanese attack at Pearl Harbor. Now docked at Pier Five as part of Historic Ships in Baltimore, there's a ceremony on the *Taney* to commemorate Pearl Harbor each year on December 7.

Lightship Chesapeake *(opposite bottom)*

With her name emblazoned boldly in white on her red hull, *Chesapeake* is docked on Pier Three before one of the glass pyramids of the National Aquarium. Commissioned in 1930, she served in the US Coast Guard and moved to Baltimore in 1982. She's a favorite of live television broadcasts.

Hanover Street Bridge

It's peaceful on the Middle Branch of the Patapsco River as the morning sun strikes the Hanover Street Bridge, with the city in the distance. This beautiful Beaux-Arts bridge was built in 1916 and features a drawbridge span in the center. It connects South Baltimore to Cherry Hill and Brooklyn.

SS John W. Brown (top)

Of the 2,710 Liberty ships built in World War II, the *John W. Brown* is one of only two surviving today. Built in Baltimore in 1942, she is still operational and often sails out to the Chesapeake Bay to reenact battles with a German Messerschmitt or a Japanese Zero.

Baltimore Harbor (bottom)

College sailing teams compete on International 420 sailboats in the Baltimore Harbor here, with a cargo ship offloading in the background. Sailing in small craft here is definitely not for the faint of heart. You're dodging tankers, pilot boats, motor boats, and regattas.

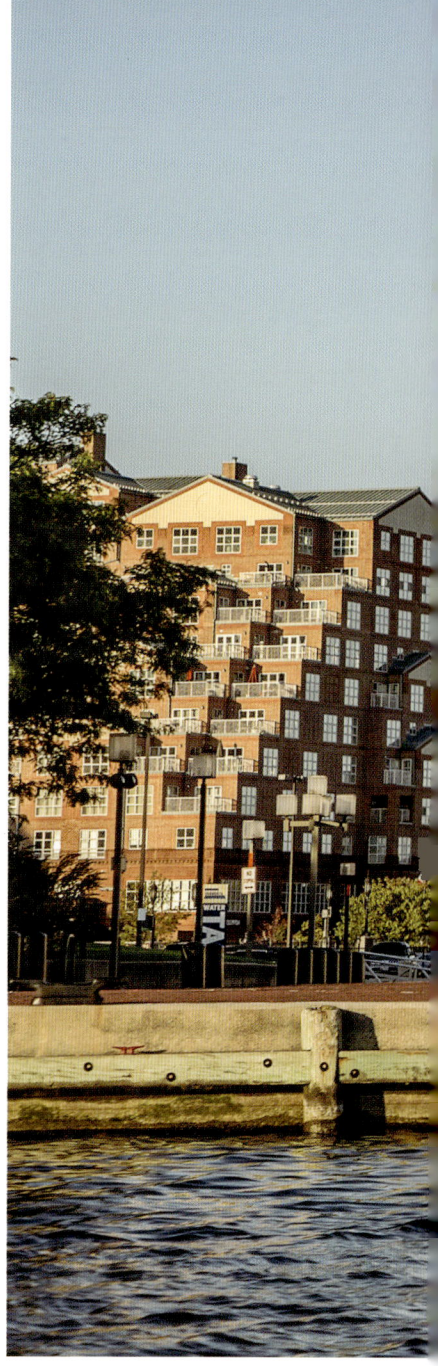

Baltimore Harbor *(top and bottom)*

The water can be choppy and the winds fluky, particularly around the Domino Sugar plant, seen here at sunset. Domino has been refining sugar in Baltimore for over ninety years and the enormous neon "Domino Sugars" sign is a Baltimore icon. You can smell the sugar when it's being processed.

Seven Foot Knoll Lighthouse *(above)*

Perched on Pier Five in the Inner Harbor, this bright red screw-pile lighthouse was built in 1855 to mark the shoals at Seven Foot Knoll on the Patapsco River. The lighthouse was home to the lightkeeper and his family. You can explore their living and working quarters today.

Skyline *(pages 56–57)*

Dusk in Baltimore is magical as the city lights reflect off the water and the sun fades to the west. This is a great time for a water taxi ride, an evening cruise, or a stroll around the promenade that surrounds Harborplace to take in the view.

Port Discovery

Families flock to this enormous children's museum in what was once Baltimore's Fish Market. Today's 80,000 square-foot building was built after the Great Fire of 1904 and includes three floors of exhibit space where children climb, play and learn — and adults are welcome to explore, too.

A Blend of Past and Present

There's a juxtaposition of old and new at this park honoring Frederick Douglass, Isaac Meyers, and African-American maritime history. The Living Classrooms has its headquarters and a restaurant in the modern building. The historic warehouse has been restored with a boat shop that uses the maritime railroad.

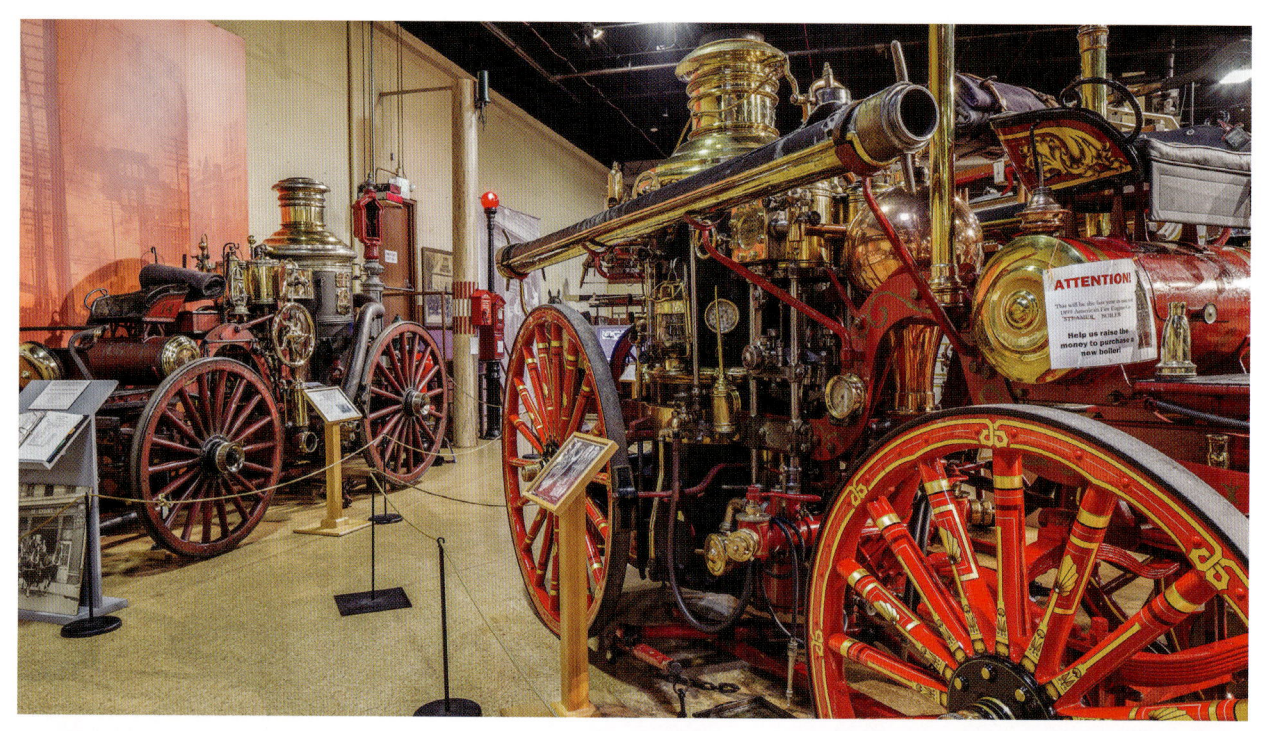

Fire Museum of Maryland (top and bottom)

With more than 40 vehicles in pristine condition, including this 1878 hand-drawn steamer and this 1926 pumper, the Fire Museum of Maryland tells the history of fire fighting in America. Just north of the city in Lutherville, you will also find a great research center there, too.

Baltimore Fire Museum (opposite)

Engine House No. 6 is unique with its six-story, 103-foot, bell-and-clock tower. Built in 1853 from cast iron, it was copied from Giotto's Campanile in Florence. Firemen from Number Six fought the Great Fire of 1904 and the station served as an emergency hospital during the fire.

Reginald F. Lewis Museum
(above and left)

Dedicated to "Maryland African-American History and Culture," this 82,000 square-foot museum opened in 2005, providing excellent space for exhibits, events, and education. The museum is named for benefactor Reginald F. Lewis, a Baltimore native and the first African-American CEO of a Fortune 500 company.

Reginald F. Lewis Museum

(above and right)

Exhibits explore slavery, segregation and discrimination, as well as contributions of African-Americans to every facet of life in Maryland from the colony's founding to present day. The museum also celebrates African-American heroes such as statesman and civil rights activist Frederick Douglass and Harriet Tubman, who were instrumental in the Underground Railroad.

63

The National Great Blacks in Wax Museum *(top and bottom)*

Life-size wax figures of Reverend Martin Luther King, Jr. and his Civil Rights Movement colleagues, along with scenes from Colonial America, make history come to life. This is the only wax museum in Baltimore and the first African-American wax museum in the nation.

Civil War Museum *(top and bottom)*

These exhibits tell the story of events that took place at President Street Station: the Baltimore Riot of 1861. As Union troops marched from President Street Station to Camden Station, Abraham Lincoln traveled a "secret passage" through Baltimore to avoid assassination en route to his inauguration in 1861.

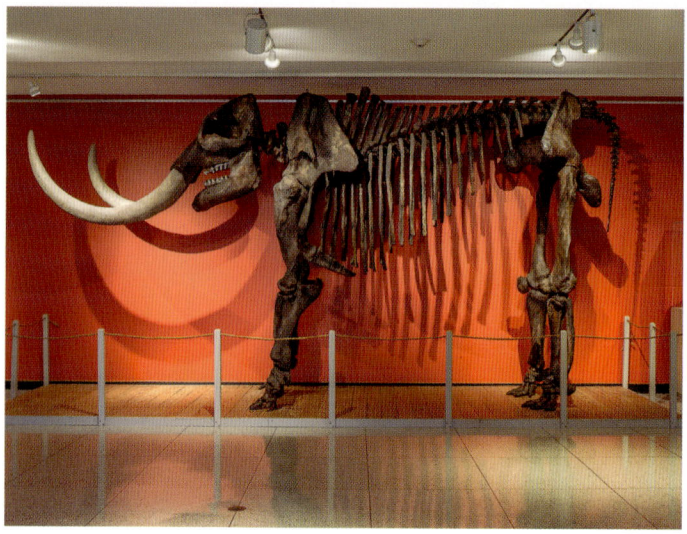

Maryland Historical Society

(top and bottom)

Since 1844, the society has been preserving and exhibiting treasures related to Maryland's history, including clothing, furniture, and natural artifacts. The collection includes Francis Scott Key's original manuscript of *The Star-Spangled Banner*.

The Star-Spangled Banner Flag House
(above and right)

Here in this small 1793 home, Mary Pickersgill sewed the enormous flag that flew over Fort McHenry during the 1814 Battle of Baltimore and inspired Francis Scott Key to write *The Star-Spangled Banner*. Visit her home and the new museum about the flag and life in the 1800s.

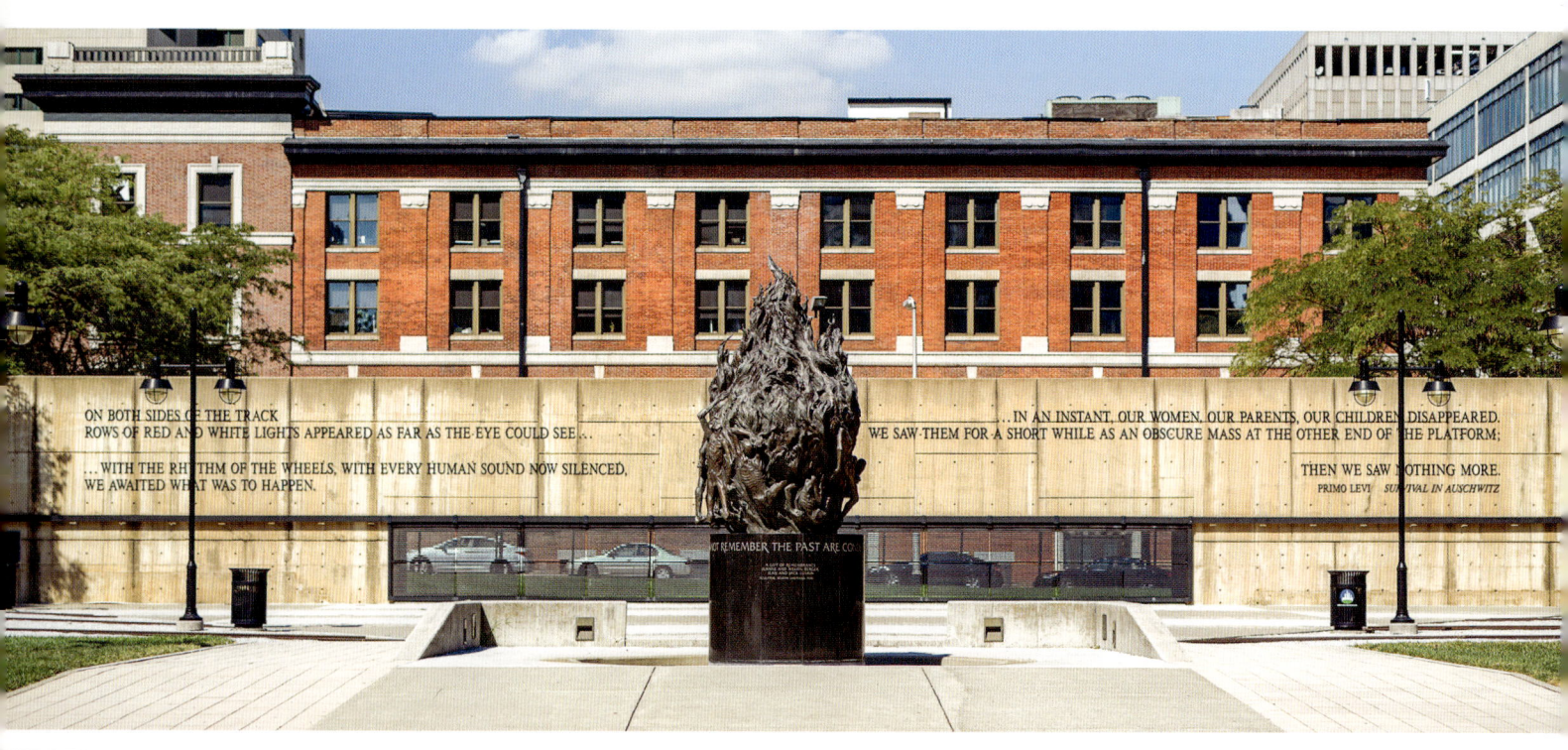

Holocaust Memorial *(top)*

Monolithic concrete slabs and railroad tracks call to mind the trains the Nazis used to transport their victims to the death camps in this moving memorial to the Jews and others exterminated during World War II. Joseph Sheppard's chilling bronze of a flame of death was added in 1988.

Jewish Museum of Maryland *(bottom)*

In 1960, Baltimore's Jewish community founded the Jewish Museum to preserve the historic synagogues in this neighborhood, the center of Jewish immigrant life in the early 1900s. The Jewish Museum focuses on the Jewish experience in Maryland and produces meaningful and thoughtful exhibits and events.

Jewish Museum of Maryland

(top and bottom)

The Jewish Museum of Maryland specializes in exhibits about life on nearby Lombard Street, over the course of the twentieth-century. These exhibits feature every-day objects and every-day people, including discussion of food, providing a real flavor of the times and culture.

69

George Peabody Library *(above and opposite)*

Architect Edmund G. Lind designed this breathtaking library with five tiers of ornamental cast-iron balconies to hold 300,000 books and provide plenty of natural light. Plus it was fire proof and climate controlled. Opened in 1878, the library was part of the Peabody Institute, founded by philanthropist George Peabody.

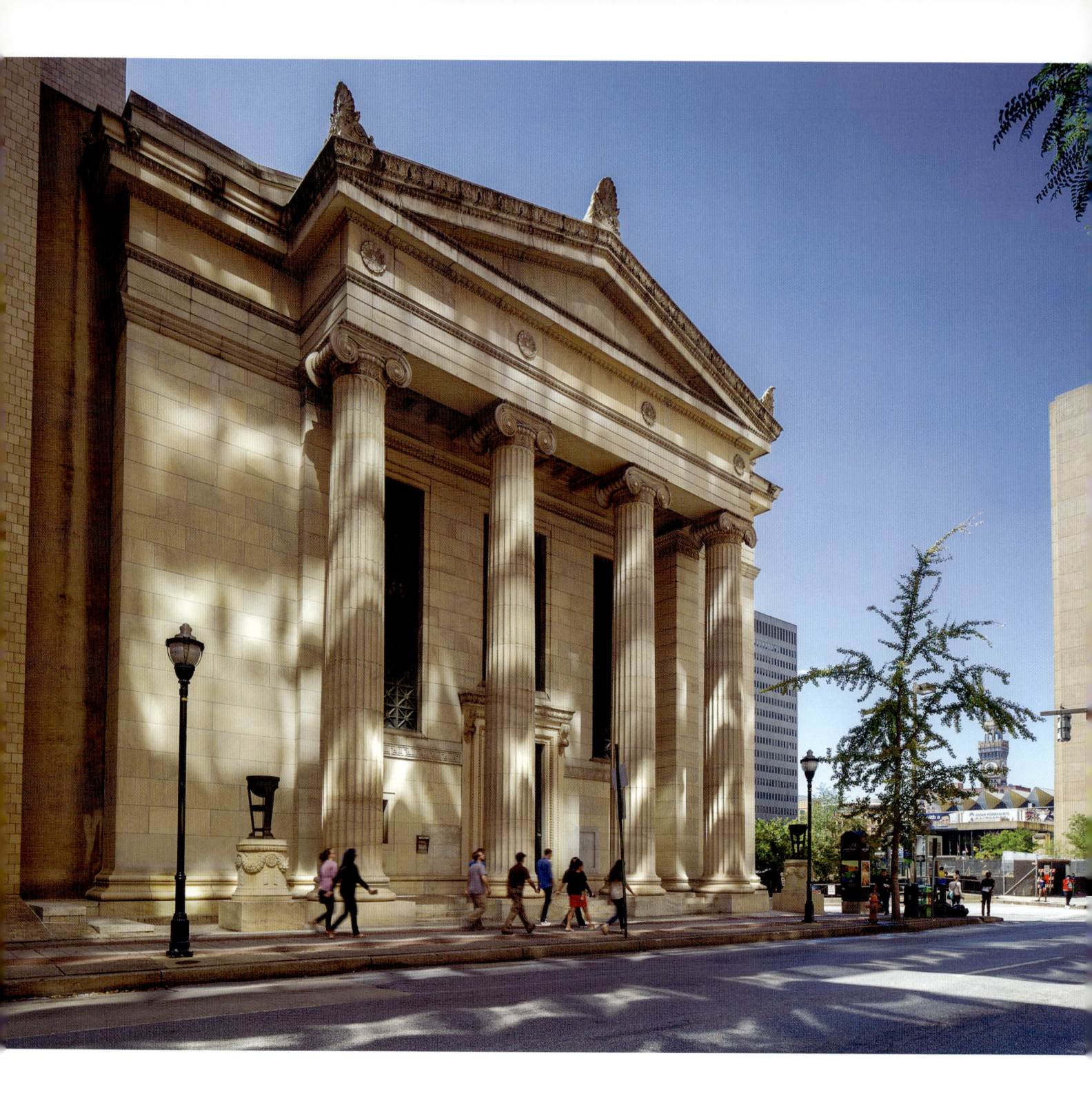

Savings Bank of Baltimore

The Great Baltimore Fire razed most of the city in 1904 and the Savings Bank of Baltimore moved its headquarters to this enormous "Temple of Thrift" at the corner of South Charles and Baltimore in 1907. Clad in white marble with Ionic columns, this Beaux-Arts masterpiece is now offices.

Thurgood Marshall Statue

This larger-than-life bronze of the first African-American Supreme Court justice stands outside the Federal Courthouse on Lombard Street. A Baltimore native, Thurgood Marshall served on the Supreme Court from 1967 to 1991. This eight-foot seven-inch statue by Reuben Kramer was unveiled in 1980.

Fells Point (*above and right*)

These brick row houses along the waterfront on Thames Street have been pubs, shops, and hotels since the 1770s. The Horse You Came In On Saloon calls itself "the oldest continually operating saloon in America." Edgar Allan Poe reported to have frequented this spot.

Fell's Point *(top and bottom)*

Eighteenth-century row houses and converted warehouses add to Fell's Point's charm, perhaps best appreciated by boat. Founded by William Fell in 1730, Fell's Point was the original deep-water harbor for Baltimore and a center for ship building and trade. The waterfront remains a popular attraction today.

Billie Holiday Statue *(opposite)*

In a strapless gown with her signature gardenias, "Lady Day" sings the blues in this elegant statue by James Earl Reid. Billie Holiday grew up here and performed in clubs on Pennsylvania Avenue. Her obituary claimed Baltimore as her birthplace but Holiday was actually born in Philadelphia in 1915.

Frank Zappa Bust *(above)*

This music iconoclast was born in Baltimore in 1940 and his bust by Lithuanian sculptor Konstantinas Bogdanas was a gift to Zappa's hometown from ardent fans in Vilnius, where a larger version is now a major tourist attraction. The bust is displayed on a twelve-foot column in Highlandtown.

Center Stage *(above)*

Founded in 1963, Center Stage moved to North Calvert Street after a fire in 1974. Previously home to Loyola College and High School, elements of the building's Jesuit roots remain, including the painted stained glass in the Nancy Roche Chapel Bar. Center Stage's productions are nationally acclaimed.

Hippodrome Theatre *(opposite)*

This jewel of a theatre was restored to its former glory in 2004 and is part of the France-Merrick Performing Arts Center. Designed by Thomas Lamb, the Hippodrome was both a vaudeville house and movie theater when it opened in 1914. Today, it's the place to see Broadway shows.

The Senator Theatre *(above and left)*

This art deco movie theatre on York Road in Towson gleams once again after extensive renovations restored it to its former glory, inside and out. The Senator wowed movie patrons with its circular lobby when it opened in 1939 and does so again today, now featuring three screens.

Everyman Theatre

Founded in 1990, Everyman Theatre moved into its new home in 2013. Built in 1910, it was originally a vaudeville house called "The Empire" and architects were delighted to uncover the "E" on the pediment peak during restoration. Its previous incarnations were as a parking garage and movie theater.

Power Plant Live *(above)*

This downtown entertainment mecca bustles with restaurants, music venues, and outside seating that's enjoyed year round. This area used to be Baltimore's wholesale food district and the old fish market is now Port Discovery Children's Museum. The enormous fountain was a gift to the city in 1907.

Power Plant *(opposite)*

Neon lights reflect into the Jones Falls from the former Pratt Street Power Plant which generated electricity for Baltimore's streetcars in the early 1900s. Today, it's an enormous Barnes & Noble bookshop flanked by restaurants floating on barges. The guitar strings actually move on the Hard Rock Café sign.

Pier Six Pavilion *(top)*

Since it opened in 1981, audiences have flocked to this open-air music venue for live concerts that feature a wide variety of music, from rock to jazz. Pier Six is also a popular spot for picnicking, offering a great view of the water.

The Charles Theatre *(bottom)*

Brilliant marquees and a blue neon sign welcome moviegoers to "the Charles" on a warm summer night. Baltimore's oldest movie theater opened in 1939. The red brick, Beaux-Arts Building was designed in 1892 by Jackson Gott as a streetcar barn and power plant. Today, it's a five-screen theater.

Hampden's Thirty-Fourth Street

Christmas in Hampden is its own little miracle as neighbors in this kitsch community vie with each other for the gaudiest, most outrageous, most over-the-top decorations on their homes. A holiday tradition since 1947, a visit to Hampden is a must at Christmas.

Charles Village (*above and opposite*)

From 1998 to 2003, the owners of these Victorian row houses competed for cash prizes to see who could paint their houses in the boldest, most exciting ways. Known as "the Painted Ladies," the brilliant color schemes continue today and are credited with revitalizing this neighborhood near Johns Hopkins.

Phoenix Shot Tower

Soaring 235 feet, the Phoenix Shot Tower was the tallest structure in the United States from 1828 to 1846. Workers produced gunshot here by dropping molten lead through a sieve at the top of the tower into a vat of water below. Centrifugal force took care of the rest.

Male/Female *(top)*

Jonathan Borofsky's *Male/Female* has dominated the plaza in front of Baltimore's Penn Station since 2004. Still controversial, this 51-foot-tall sculpture is made of intersecting aluminum male and female silhouettes sharing a neon heart. It's a stark contrast to the Beaux-Arts train station and period street lamps.

Penn Station *(bottom)*

An aerial view provides a unique perspective of Penn Station and *Male/Female*. Designed by Kenneth MacKenzie Murchison for the Pennsylvania Railroad, it was the height of elegance and technology when it opened in 1911. Among Amtrak's busiest stations, it underwent major renovations in the 1980s.

Panorama *(pages 92–93)*

Facing north, Baltimore's waterfront glows at dusk with Piers Three through Six punctuating the water and reflections from the National Aquarium and Pier Six Pavilion. To the east are the office towers and residences of thriving Harbor East. To the west is the glowing promenade of the Ritz-Carlton Residences.

Baltimore City College *(opposite)*

This Gothic-style building with a 151-foot-tall tower, complete with turrets and gargoyles, has been home to Baltimore City High School since 1928. Founded in 1839, "City College" is the third oldest public high school in the United States. Today, it's a magnet school offering the International Baccalaureate.

Johns Hopkins Hospital *(above)*

Perched high on a hill, Johns Hopkins Hospital opened in this Queen Anne-style building in 1889 and its dome is a symbol for the world-renowned medical institution today. When it opened, Hopkins was the largest hospital in the country with cutting-edge technology. That tradition continues today.

US Lacrosse Museum *(top and bottom)*

Maryland has always been a hub of lacrosse and where better to learn about the sport than this museum run by U.S. Lacrosse? From its Native American roots through today, museum exhibits include helmets, sticks, balls and uniforms as well as the National Lacrosse Hall of Fame.

Johns Hopkins University

Students enjoy this lush, green quadrangle and magnificent shade trees in front of Shriver Hall. The university moved here to the Homewood Campus in 1916. The quadrangles, crossed with red brick paths, have been a signature of the handsome campus design.

Towson University

Towson students have loved Stephens Hall's cupola and chiming clock since the university opened its doors here in 1915. Douglas H. Thomas, Jr. designed this Jacobean-styled building after Blickling Hall, an English manor house where King Henry VIII's second wife Anne Boleyn once lived.

Notre Dame of Maryland University

Gibbons Hall's bell tower and gold cross soar against a brilliant blue sky on an autumn day. Notre Dame moved to this red-brick building, reminiscent of other great American colleges and universities, in 1873. It is still the centerpiece of Notre Dame's Charles Street Campus.

Baltimore Polytechnic Institute *(top)*

Burkert Hall has welcomed "Poly" students since the school moved to this campus at Falls Road and Cold Spring Lane in 1967. Founded in 1883 as a boys' school, with a specialty in engineering, Poly was the first Baltimore City public school to integrate in 1952. In 1974, girls were admitted.

University of Maryland, Baltimore Campus *(bottom)*

This is an uncommonly quiet moment at UMBC's Commons, the university's center for student life since 2002. With a food court, game rooms and bookstore, the Commons is a great place to chill. The terrace and steps down to the grassy quad are favorite hangout spots, too.

University of Baltimore *(opposite)*

The John and Frances Angelos Law Center opened in this multi-faceted, multi-textured building in 2013. Designed by German architect Stefan Behnisch, following an international design competition in 2008, this twelve-story building takes maximum advantage of every bit of space on its triangular single-acre lot.

JOHN AND FRANCES ANGELOS LAW CENTER
UNIVERSITY OF BALTIMORE

MT. ROYAL AVE.

FlowerMart

Mount Vernon United Methodist Church provides a stunning backdrop for FlowerMart. This Baltimore rite of spring has been a tradition since 1911. Held during the first weekend in May, festivities include hat contests, maypole dancing, and peppermint sticks stuck in lemons, also known as "Baltimore Lemon Sticks."

Cathedral of Mary Our Queen

Roman Catholics have been worshipping at this huge Neo-Gothic cathedral since 1959. It's the third-largest cathedral in the United States and the co-seat of the Archbishop of Baltimore. The Baltimore Archdiocese is the oldest in the country, founded in 1789.

Baltimore Basilica *(above and left)*

This is the first Roman Catholic cathedral in America, built between 1806 and 1821 and designed by Benjamin Henry Latrobe, best known for his work on the US Capitol. Many call the basilica Latrobe's greatest masterpiece with its magnificent dome and skylights that bathe the basilica in sunlight.

Baltimore Basilica

Light streams into the basilica's nave from the side windows, illuminating the pale yellow, rose and blue on the walls. The basilica's interior was restored to its original colors amongst extensive renovations completed in 2006, in honor of the 200th anniversary of breaking ground on the site.

Green Mount Cemetery *(above)*

The spire of the Green Mount Chapel kisses the sky on a breezy day in this historic cemetery, dedicated in 1839. The cemetery's list of grave sites reads like a "Who's Who" of Baltimore including Johns Hopkins, Enoch Pratt, Henry and William Walters, as well as John Wilkes Booth.

Lovely Lane United Methodist Church *(opposite)*

This magnificent Romanesque building by architect Stanford White was inspired by the twelfth-century Santa Maria of Pomposa in Northern Italy. Known as "the Mother Church of American Methodism," the Lovely Lane congregation moved here in 1884 as it celebrated its centennial.

Mount Clare Museum House

(top and bottom)

Charles Carroll the Barrister built this splendid Georgian house on his country plantation in 1760. Today, it is Baltimore's oldest residence. The museum, maintained by the Colonial Dames, has beautifully appointed rooms that offer a glimpse into late eighteenth-century life.

Maryvale Castle

Dr. and Mrs. Walter F. Wickes moved their family to this Tudor-style "castle" in the Greenspring Valley in 1916. Modeled after Warwick Castle in England, with a Great Hall and 65 rooms, it was among the area's biggest residences, now home to Maryvale Preparatory School, an independent Catholic girls school.

Tuscany-Canterbury *(above and left)*

Architect Clyde Nelson Friz developed these Italian Renaissance-style apartment buildings from 1915 to 1918. A century on, The Lombardy and The Tuscany still add elegance to this beautifully landscaped neighborhood. Friz would appreciate how the trees have matured around the buildings.

Tuscany-Canterbury

Spring in Tuscany-Canterbury is a treat with blossoming trees and lovingly tended gardens, like this one in front of a distinctive, Tudor-style home. This is one of many Baltimore neighborhoods where residents are passionate about their history, architecture, and community.

Evergreen Museum & Library

This elegantly manicured Italian garden at Evergreen expands behind the Gilden Age mansion that was home to two generations of the Garrett family from 1878 to 1942. The Garretts donated Evergreen House to Johns Hopkins University in 1952. It's now a museum, hosting events and weddings in the garden once again.

Evergreen Museum & Library
(top and bottom)

The Italianate portico of Evergreen House makes a dramatic impression in yellow against a blue sky. B&O Railroad magnates John Work Garrett and son T. Harrison Garrett lived here with their families. It houses over 50,000 pieces, including the world's largest collection of Tiffany glass.

Carroll Museum

This is the back garden of Charles Carroll of Carollton's mansion on Lombard Street, where he lived in the 1820s. Carroll died here at age 95 in 1832, the last surviving signer of the "Declaration of Independence." This was reported to be the largest and most expensive house in town.

Homewood Museum *(above and right)*

Charles Carroll, Jr. received Homewood Estate as a wedding gift from his father Charles Carroll of Carrollton in 1800. He designed and built this mansion from 1801 to 1808. Today, it is a museum at the heart of Johns Hopkins University's "Homewood Campus" exhibiting eighteenth-century period furnishings.

Dickeyville *(above and left)*

From red clapboard to stone and brick, the houses in Dickeyville are a delightful assortment of materials, styles, and ages. Full of history and local lore, Dickeyville is a tight-knit community just within the city limits along the Gwynns Falls, which powered the mills when it was settled.

Patterson Park

This boldly painted Victorian-style pagoda, on the peak of Patterson Park, is especially enchanting in spring. Designed by Charles H. Latrobe in 1890, you can climb the pagoda again today thanks to a major renovation completed in 2002 which also helped revive the now thriving Patterson Park community.

Sherwood Gardens *(above and left)*

The colorful tulips and flowering trees in Sherwood Gardens are spectacular at the end of April and beginning of May. John W. Sherwood began planting tulips here in the 1920s and now it's the most famous tulip garden in North America. Some 80,000 tulip bulbs are planted each year.

Cylburn Arboretum *(opposite)*

Jesse and Edyth Tyson moved to Cylburn Mansion in 1888 and planted many of the trees that continue to flourish as the Cylburn Arboretum today. Designed by George A. Frederick, architect of Baltimore City Hall, Cylburn Mansion is the centerpiece of the 207-acre park and nature preserve.

118

Druid Hill Park
(opposite, top and bottom)

Pink cherry blossoms pop along Druid Hill Reservoir here, in one of the oldest public parks in America. Druid Hill Park opened in 1860 and George A. Frederick designed the red, yellow, and green "Latrobe Pavilion" as a station for a little railway that once chugged through here.

Druid Hill Park *(above)*

Opened in 1888, this spectacular glass conservatory in Druid Hill Park is the second-oldest surviving in the country. Designed by George A. Frederick, the large Palm House has 175 windows that are 50 feet tall and an adjoining Orchid House. It's now the Howard Peter Rawlings Conservatory & Botanic Garden.

National Aquarium *(opposite top and bottom)*

Children have loved getting eye-to-eye with the fish at the National Aquarium since it opened in the Inner Harbor in 1981. Exhibits in the Glass Pavilion take you to Australia where you can discover more than 1,800 animals native to "Down Under" including crocodiles, snakes, and flying foxes.

National Aquarium *(above)*

The twelve-story Glass Pavilion of the National Aquarium opened in 2005 with the exhibit "Animal Planet Australia: Wild Extremes." When illuminated at night, one may glimpse the foliage and 53-foot waterfall, as well as the aviary within. The pavilion's peak adds interest to the Inner Harbor skyline.

The Maryland Zoo *(top and bottom)*

Penguins have always been a favorite at the Maryland Zoo and the Penguin Coast Exhibit provides a wonderfully close perspective as the penguins dive and swim and bask on the rocks. The zoo also features notable sculptures like these bronze ostrich rushing through the grass by Bart Walter.

Inner Harbor View *(top)*

Baltimore Harbor is most exciting during festivals like this with tall ships docked along the waterfront and crowds enjoying the promenade. This is also the iconic view of the Inner Harbor's skyline from the trusses of 100 East Pratt to the World Trade Center and the National Aquarium pyramid.

Pimlico Race Course *(bottom)*

Thoroughbreds thunder past, spurred on by jockeys at Pimlico Race Course. Founded in 1870, Pimlico is the second oldest track in the country and home of the Preakness Stakes, the second leg of the Triple Crown. Man o' War, Sea Biscuit, Secretariat, and Cigar all ran here.

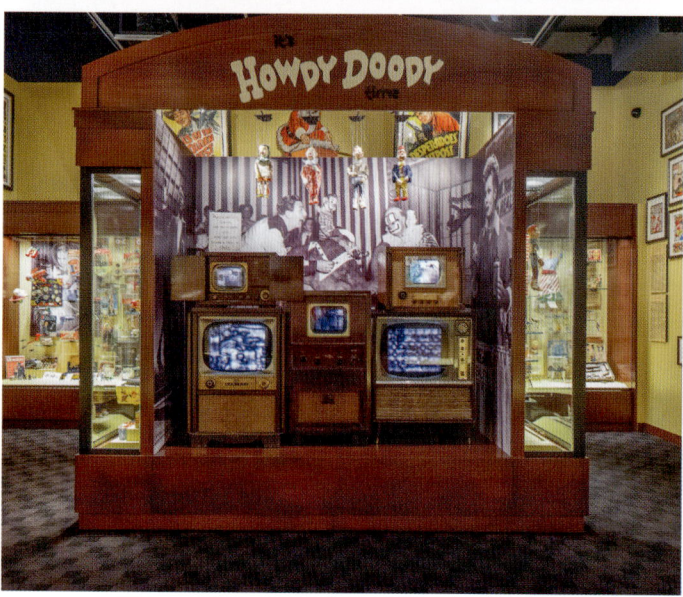

Geppi's Entertainment Museum

(top and bottom)

Bat Man, Howdy Doody, and Donald Duck are among the exhibits here at this treasure-trove comics museum. Stephen A. Geppi, president and CEO of Diamond Comics Distributors, founded and owns the museum and displays much of his own personal collection here.

Babe Ruth Birthplace *(left and right)*

George Herman "Babe" Ruth, Jr. was born in this Baltimore row house at 216 Emory Street on February 6, 1895. Today, "Babe's" home is just three blocks away from Oriole Park at Camden Yards. Exhibits include balls, bars, and memorabilia from "the Babe's" legendary career in baseball.

M&T Bank Stadium (top)

You can almost hear the roar of the fans as the Baltimore Ravens take the field at M&T Stadium. The stadium was built for Baltimore's National Football League team when it moved here in 1998. The team is named in honor of Edgar Allan Poe's poem *The Raven*.

Oriole Park at Camden Yards (bottom)

It's "batter up" at Camden Yards on a clear summer night. Baltimore's Major League Baseball team moved here on Opening Day of 1992. Previously the rail yard for the B&O Railroad's Camden Station, the former B&O Warehouse can be seen behind right field.

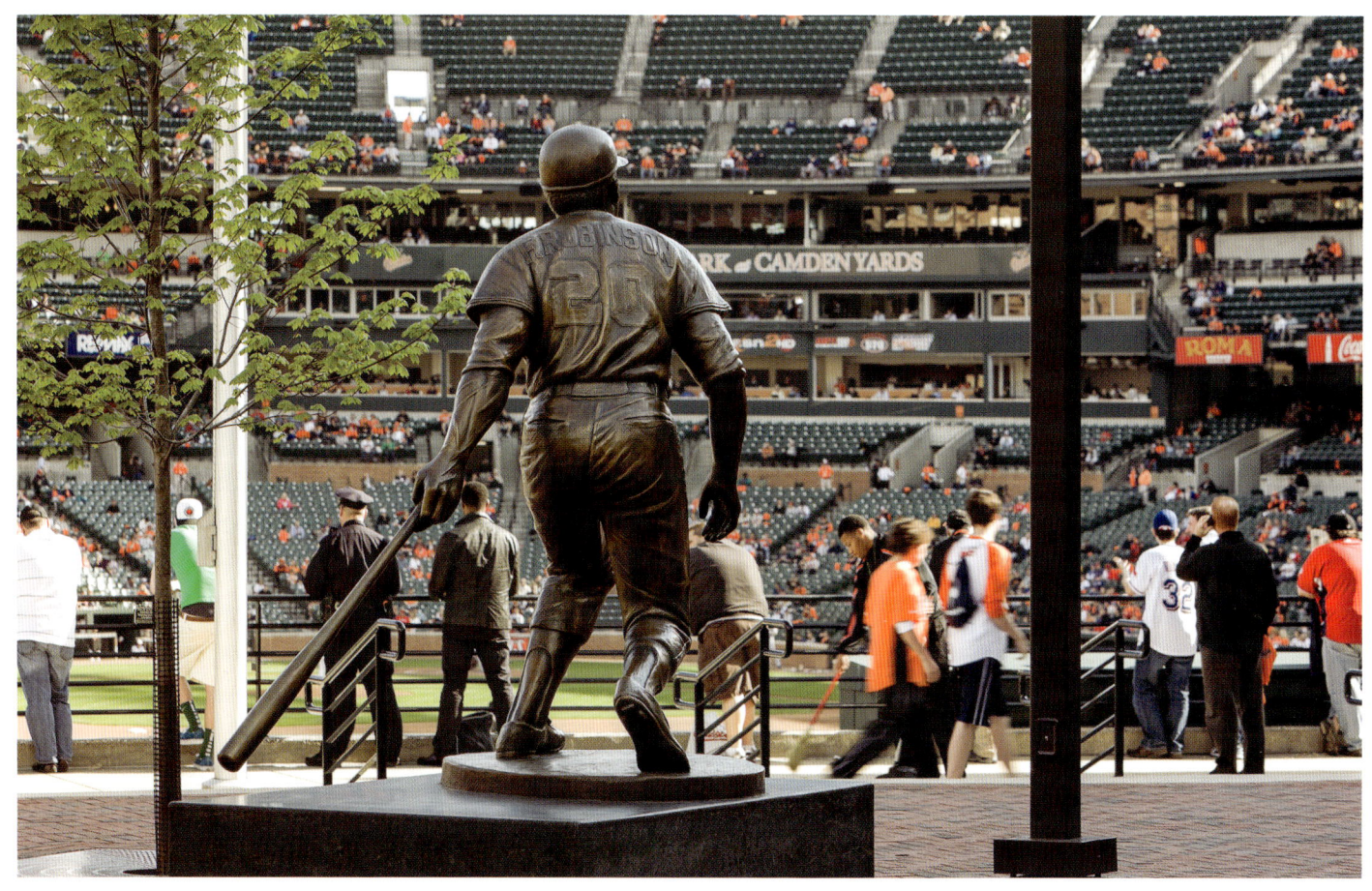

Orioles Hall of Fame Statues *(above)*

This Toby Mendez bronze captures legendary Oriole outfielder Frank Robinson, just after slugging the ball. It's one of six sculptures honoring Orioles Hall of Famers, erected at Camden Yards, to celebrate the ballpark's 20th anniversary. Teammates Frank Robinson and Brooks Robinson were the original Hall of Fame inductees in 1977.

Brooks Robinson Statue *(right)*

The great third baseman Brooks Robinson, with an appropriately golden glove, winds up to throw in this bronze by Joseph Sheppard. Robinson always wore jersey number five and played for the Orioles his entire 23-year career. The statue stands just outside Camden Yards, a favorite rendezvous site for fans.

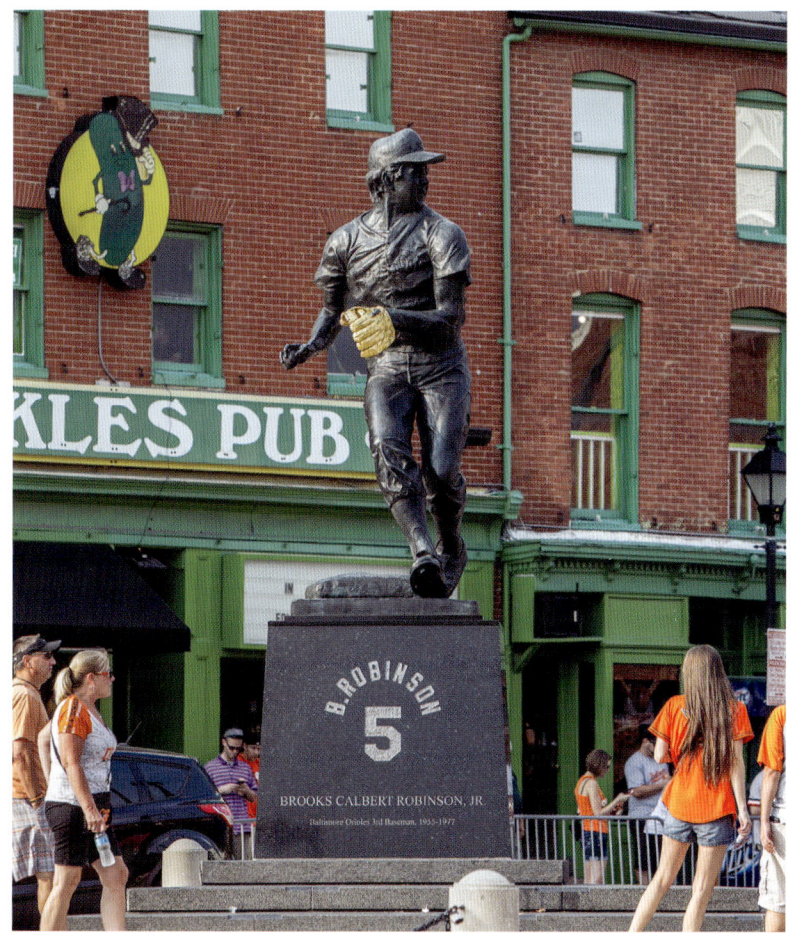

Alan Gilbert

New Jersey born, Alan was raised in Baltimore's Mount Washington neighborhood. He attended Baltimore City College for high school, followed by the University of Wisconsin and graduate work at Maryland Institute of Art.

Alan's career as a corporate assignment photographer spans over thirty years. Architecture, interiors, and gardens and portraits are his favored subjects. His work has helped his clients grow their businesses and win many awards for excellence in their fields.

In the late 1990s, Alan and his wife Nancy embraced new digital technology, founding DOC Baltimore, a digital services and print specialty studio serving the art and design community. Working from their studio workshop in Baltimore's Hampden neighborhood, Alan works with many of Baltimore's leading artists and cultural institutions.

Brooke McDonald

Brooke is a filmmaker and writer who has worked for CNN, Bloomberg, and Reuters. From Baltimore-based Houpla, Inc., Brooke and her husband and partner Michael Brassert produce documentaries, commercials, and websites. They also consult on content creation as well as train journalists internationally. Brooke began her career as a newspaper reporter for the Sentinel Newspapers and producer for Maryland Public Television. Born and raised in Baltimore, Brooke holds a BA from Duke University and an MA from Cornell.